The Many Paths I Followed.

By Philip R. Gosling

Copyright © 2023 Philip Gosling

ISBN: 978-1-77422-158-7

All rights reserved. No part of this work may be reproduced or used in any form, except brief passages in reviews, without prior written permission of the author.

Printed in Canada.

TABLE of CONTENTS

Part 1. "The Early Years"

1.	My Family and the Coldstream Guards	3
2.	Departure England, Arrival Canada	11
3.	Real Estate Highlights	15
4.	Clairfields – A Developer's Journey	25
5.	Wellington County Brewery	31

Part 2. "The Mission"

6.	Nature. Protect and Preserve	47
7.	My Bruce Trail Story	53
8.	The Gosling Foundation	83
9.	GRIPP. Gosling Research Institute for Plant Preservation, University of Guelph.	91
10.	The Tree Haven Project	97

Introduction: Why Write a Book

You know life can be an interesting journey, well worth recording—if it serves some useful purpose.

My sister believed in horoscopes and told me I was lucky to be a "Leo" (lion) a natural leader, born in August, known for its roar, taking action, and 'self-rated' opinions. Well, that's me, I must admit.

I stepped out, applied my native-born business instincts, learning by doing, and seizing opportunities wherever my path led me.

Anyway I like to write, and now, in my senior years, it gives me pleasure and satisfaction such as I often laugh to myself as I recall those special memories.

.

To live longer and be happy... write a book.!

Foreword

by Ross Maclean, author of *The Fascination of the Bruce Peninsula and the Bruce Trail, 2004.*

When Philip told me he was writing his memoirs I never doubted he would 'just do it'. This is his mantra.

His story is of a remarkable passage of time in a life of discovery, personal growth and change, part memoir and part reality, from business success to a deeply felt love of natural life whether nurturing his home garden or protecting the lands and forests of the Niagara Escarpment.

As a founder of the Bruce Trail and his leadership in its building, by volunteers in one year in 1962, he will be his best remembered by Ontarians.

In notable recognition of his many achievements and philanthropy are his Awards of the Order of Canada and Hon LLD. from the University of Guelph.

Part One
EARLY YEARS

MY FAMILY and the COLDSTREAM GUARDS

Fred Gosling and Winifred Beatrice Oakley (Mom and Dad)

Me and my sister outside Dad's Removal company

MY FAMILY AND THE COLDSTREAM GUARDS

My Father (Fred) was the first in the family to immigrate to Canada. In 50's 'Go West Young Man' was the slogan at that time. He travelled by ship from Liverpool to Halifax and then by train to a logging camp 'up North' to Winnipeg. You bet, after a few shifts he moved to an easier job at Eaton's Department store, downtown Winnipeg and, as he often told us kids, evenings at the Fort Garry Horse Hotel.

When news of the first world war arrived in Canada, he and many of his new immigrant friends enlisted and promptly sailed back to Liverpool in England. He never spoke of his war experience, but upon his demob he joined his father's new garden business where, one day, he met my mother, who like many young girls at that time, fell for the handsome young man in uniform. My mother had a good education and was an accomplished pianist. My Father was seen as a 'working man' with a good instinct for business.

I was the 4th of 5 children, Bernard and Norma being the eldest, both served in the British Army in the Middle East. Len, the middle brother, a student engineer, was in training for the R.A.F. I was 13 when I left school to assist my father, who by then had started a removal business and was needing help (with my brothers away). I learned how to rope up a piano and lower it through a window down three stories to his van. It was amazing how he did this. Then his trick was to keep the piano off to one side until he got paid for the removal and, if payment was delayed, he would reload the instrument in the van, where it often stayed for days or got dumped in our front room at home. (At times there would be 2 or 3 pianos FOR SALE...on which I could practice my boogie-woogie). Eventually at age 17, charged with patriotic fervor of wartime, I was old enough to volunteer for the oldest and most 'elite' British Army regiment, the Coldstream Guards.

"I caught a train from Birmingham and a bus to the Guards Depot at Caterham, Surrey to begin training..."

Changing of the Guard at Buckingham Palace

The Royal Wedding November 20th 1947

LIFE AND TRAINING OF A GUARDSMAN

Having enlisted, without telling my parents, and signed up for 5 years active and 7 reserve service, at age 17 years, I caught a train from Birmingham to London and bus to the Guards Depot at Caterham, Surrey to begin training with about 20 other recruits. It was hard going getting up before reveille, scrubbing floors and out on the Parade ground where the three-stripe drill instructor, with his pace measuring cane, threatened various forms of torture if we recruits slowed or failed to meet his command. This intensive training lasted 12 to 16 weeks during which time about 4 of our group got moved out to 'service' corps…including one man who threw down his rifle and questioned the Sgt's parentage. As we left this tough challenge…(you know I got to like the competition of the 7-mile cross country runs and I enjoyed playing boogie-woogie on the N.A.F.F.I. piano as well as songs by ear.)

I remember felling proud when we 'passed out' (paraded) in perfect step before the Depot's Commander. Then it was onto field training at Purbright Station in Wales, where I remember, on a field exercise, as a promising platoon leader, I tripped on a tree root, fired off a round of blanks on my sten gun and spent a night in jail.

In 1946/47 I was in #2 company of the Coldstream Guards stationed in London at the Wellington Barracks, across from Buckingham Palace. We were on guard/sentry duties both outside and inside the palace gates for about a year during which time the regiment was on duty for the WEDDING OF THE QUEEN (then a princess) to the future DUKE OF EDINBURGH…PRINCE PHILIP. I was on duty in the 'ROYAL MALL' along with the cheering crowds.

It was truly a once in a life memory of the Queen's marriage 70 years ago.

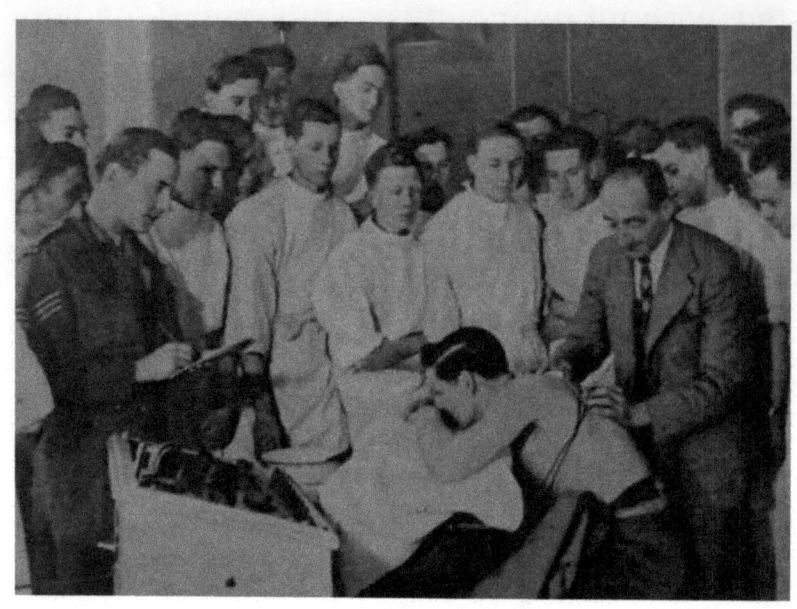

"I attended the Army School of Physical Therapy at Netely, Hampshire on the south coast"

Demobbed on on my way back home...

Later, on an overseas posting from Southampton, #2 company was on board a converted troop ship, sailing through stormy waters (almost everyone was sick) for about 7 days of swinging hammocks, hooked on beams, in the hold, to Palestine in the Middle East. It was here, on patrol, that I experienced being under fire for the first time.

We were first housed in a half built 8 storey apartment building (for peace keeping) and when on the roof, we were under fire from two sides and firing back when it got too close. I remember sneaking down to the ground floor and joining a huddle of Arab tribesmen drinking strong and very sweet coffee in tiny cups. Using hand signals, we traded names, "You Mustafa...Me Wronald" (I never could pronounce my rrrrrs). I gave up trying, and this is when I adopted 'PHILIP', as per the very recent memory involving the royal Philip, and have been PHILIP ever since.

A few months later, while escorting the Irish Guards military band on tour near Bethlehem, our couch was ambushed and as escorts we were ordered to clear a path. We were getting fired on and I got badly hurt by a rock fall set off by local tribesmen (an incident referred to later). Several musicians were injured amid the frantic efforts to escape the firing.

Another time the whole company toured through Israel in our military vehicles...the purpose we were told, was 'showing the colour', that we were there to keep the peace. In some places we were cheered and others we got rocks thrown at us...to which we troopers responded in the usual 'British way', which was not the V for Victory.

Eventually, the British Mandate over, we were shipped, via Suez, to Tobruk, Libya, where I suffered a second accident. On a recreation weekend at a swimming pool, I dived off a high tower and hit head to head with a swimmer coming up for air. Suffering severe headaches, I reported sick, and while waiting to see a doctor, I happened to pick up a magazine and read about the 'Army School of Physiotherapy' in the U.K. WOW! I was immediately excited at the prospect of education and training, and I saw a Path to a promising future. It took a while (and a lot of nerve) to ask for a transfer, but I remember addressing the Colonel of the Regiment, (I can see him now looking at this young, blue-eyed boy, like a wise old grandfather). He saw my youth and enthusiasm and approved my transfer to a Medical Corps Hospital in Egypt (a rare happening).

I billeted at a military hospital in Ismailia (by the Suez Canal...no swimming allowed) for a year as a medic and then, endured, survived another troop ship sailing back to England, where I happily attended the Army School of Physical Therapy at Netley, Hampshire on the south coast of England.

In the next 1-2 years of concentrated effort, (I knew I was lucky to be there) I was able to win FIRST CLASS CERTIFICATES in Education and Sports Physiotherapy, which on my demob (rank corporal...just like my dad) with a little outside support, helped me to win entrance to the School of Physiotherapy at the University of Birmingham. Later I became a chartered member of the society MCSP.

Note: My brother Len settled in Canada, married Margaret and had five children...all boys. My younger sister Rita married in Canada and had one child.

DEPARTING ENGLAND
APRIL 1955

DEPART ENGLAND. ARRIVAL CANADA.

**I took the Victory sign as a good omen
for my future success in Canada**

4th of April 1955 I left for Canada

DEPARTURE ENGLAND, ARRIVAL CANADA

NO SMALL SHIP! I boarded the Queen Elizabeth Liner, docked at Southampton—'on the Channel' ready for its regular sailing to New York. On arrival, my first memory of America was seeing 'monster cars' with huge tail fins on the nearby freeway (Wow!). Leaving the ship, I joined other immigrants gathered at the Grand Central train station and from there travelled by train to Niagara Falls where we had our immigration papers stamped by a welcoming officer and then...it was on to Toronto.

But an event happened before I left England.

With a day to spare before embarking, I wandered through the famous parks and places I had come to know when on royal guard duties many years previously. Without planning it I found myself on Downing Street and had joined a knot of visitors staring at #10. Suddenly to my/our complete surprise, the front door opened and out stepped Winston Churchill—the Prime Minister. He looked over at us and gave his famous V for Victory salute. I will never forget the emotion I felt and the huge roar that came from my throat.

I took the Victory sign as a good omen for my future success in Canada.

ARRIVAL IN CANADA. EARLY APRIL 1955.

It was a very cold, unwelcoming, snow blizzardy day in Toronto

Here I was at Union Station, undeterred by the freezing cold, just happy to be on new ground and on my way to 'fame and fortune'.

With a little guidance, I located and then rented a room in an attic in the mid-town for $8.00 a week. Wasting no time...I spotted a 'help wanted' advert in a local newspaper for a salesman. The address was nearby so 'why not'. I walked there and met with the Sales Manager. He asked me, "how long have you been in Canada". I told him about 10 hours—not impressed, he told me to come back once I knew the value of a dollar. I left in a huff, not realizing the job was in Real Estate sales—a Path for me—yet to be determined.

There followed a dozen failed attempts at selling household appliances and other goods door-to-door. I was almost out of cash (even had an interview for a Flying Officer physiotherapy position with the Canadian Air Force) but backed off...I had other ideas of self-employment. Anyway, at that time I began thinking of a temporary fix and reluctantly called the Canadian Physiotherapy Office in Toronto and was advised to contact St. Joseph's Hospital in Guelph. I phoned first, then, being broke, hitchhiked my way along busy highways to keep an appointment by NOON...the next day...what pressure! Anyway I was hired, as a temporary (promising to help find a replacement) and with a small cash advance was able to buy a bus ticket back to Toronto, pick up my suitcase and return to Guelph, where I found local lodgings close to the hospital.

After a few months and by now feeling very unsettled "as if by magic" a letter arrived from the Hebrides Islands in Scotland. A fellow graduate in physiotherapy, unhappy with his posting to a remote hospital, asked if there was a possible position for him in Guelph. I quickly wrote back to say YES—there was—TAKE MINE ! In 6-8 weeks, John Flavell and his wife and child arrived, I gave him my white coat and stepped out ready to start a new career...in REAL ESTATE!

REAL ESTATE
HIGHLIGHTS 1956-2022

Old Customs House on St. George's Square

One day at the office, I spotted a notice in the Guelph Guardian newspaper (June 1960). The Old Customs House on St. Georges Square was for sale.

TOP BID FOR CUSTOMS BUILDING

PHILLIP GOSLING

It was announced today by Phillip Gosling and Albert Fish, officials of Tri-County Holdings Limited, the highest bidder on the former Customs building, that they are awaiting an out of town engineers report before making a final decision on the future of the old building.

They have apparently been considering the advantages and the many disadvantages of maintaining the old structure and are wondering if over a period of time the best interests of the City will, in fact, be served by the preservation of the old structure.

REAL ESTATE HIGHLIGHTS

"I seized opportunities that others missed"

Beginning in sales with Albert Fish Real Estate, I soon learned the trade—I worked hard for long hours, and found getting paid by commission on results 'never on salary' suited my personality. To advance my career, I took courses at McMaster University in Hamilton on real estate appraisals and saw commercial real estate as the main opportunity for growth in my future,. But more than that, I learned that real estate development was every city's 'engine of growth', creating incentives for forward thinking.

Four projects are selected to best represent the opportunities and challenges of development: Customs House, St George's Square; Bullfrog Mall; Evergreen Mall in Kitchener; and Clairfield's, 'a developer's journey.'

CUSTOMS HOUSE, ST GEORGE`S SQUARE, 1960.

One day at the office, I spotted a notice in the *THE GUELPH GUARDIAN* newspaper (June, 1960). The old Customs House on St George`s Square was for sale. On speculation, Albert Fish and I submitted a bid for $101,000 which, to our complete surprise, was accepted in Ottawa! At the time, our business account was at the Bank of Nova Scotia. I met with Cliff Fraliey, Branch Manager, to discuss possible funding and learned the bank would be interested in this location for a new premises. Following the manager's lead, I contacted the bank head office and, surprisingly, with little effort, negotiated the terms of a 25-year lease in a new building (Imagine that—in St George`s Square yet!). Our next move was to apply to the city for a demolition permit. Well, as you might guess, we immediately faced opposition (who are these guys?) but to keep a long story short, we had no building

HISTORY

The site of the Mall was once the southern edge of a pond that extended across Eramosa Rd. Its several acres was said to harbour the giant bullfrog whose nightly chorus both cheered and disturbed those that happened by.

The nearby Bullfrog Inn to the North, now a barber shop, was a haven for weary travellers around the turn of the century. Highway 24, now a 4 lane highway, was then a dirt road leading to Eramosa Township and points north. Farmers, merchants, and early settlers must have appreciated the warmth of the friendly roadside inn but little is recorded of their reactions to the nightly chorus from the nearby Bullfrog Pond.

But the City grew and changes occurred. The creek and the springs that fed the Pond were diverted and gradually the frogs' home was lost. Now only occasional ponding occurs in the Spring and the water so collected is neither habitable or lasts long enough for frogs.

Then man further intervened; an area was quarried for gravel, another filled with rubbish, home-owners building on firm edges pushed top soil on top of rubbish to expand their rear yards. Children, increasing in numbers, criss-crossed the area with paths. Tree houses were built, elms died of Dutch elm disease, and nature's sounds gave way to the rumbling traffic, and chain saws, trail bikes, and snowmobiles were heard for the first time.

A final change was inevitable and following several years of negotiations with the City and area residents, final plans were made.

The City acquired most of the original pond area for redesign as a storm water retention area, and the southern tip of the former pond was filled to a depth of 8 to 12 feet.

And so the course of history has unfolded in a manner hopefully understood and supported by most of this Community, but so that no one forgets that this was once a bullfrog's pond, this Centre is called

BULLFROG MALL

experience and no money, so we chose to accept an offer to purchase from the local Wolfond family for the value of the lease (a bloody give away at the price!). There is more that might be told of city politics and not having the right connections, but in the passage of time, the new 'modern' premises replaced the stately building that once faced Guelph's historic central square in older times.

BULLFROG MALL, 1970 - 1975.

One day driving around the Eramosa Road area, I noticed a vacant area across from Zellers (a former project). Apparently left behind by easier city expansion to the north, it was a low spot named by locals because of its history of bullfrogs croaking deep into the night. Surrounding this former pond area were a number of houses with deep lots. Speculating that this land had potential for a shopping center, I bought one of the houses fronting on Stevenson Street, moved in my own family, and over the next 2 years spent time acquiring options to buy the other homes—explaining to each homeowner that the high price offered (with a non-refundable cash deposit) gave me time to seek a zone change for development purposes.

Staying on course—waiting, talking with city planning and growing more confident (with a 25-year lease from A & P grocery supermarket in hand), I arranged bank loans and was anxious to confirm all the house purchases and proceed with an application to the City for a zone change to permit the shopping center—as first imagined. My plan now included the A & P (a 30,000 sq ft supermarket), a Shoppers Drug Mart, a number of local service stores and a branch of the city library.

The location, I felt, called for an attractive design of the building (later enhanced by local architect Karl Brestenski) and I was very proud when city council, after much deliberation, gave its approval and construction could start, but then the unexpected happened!

REAL ESTATE HIGHLIGHTS

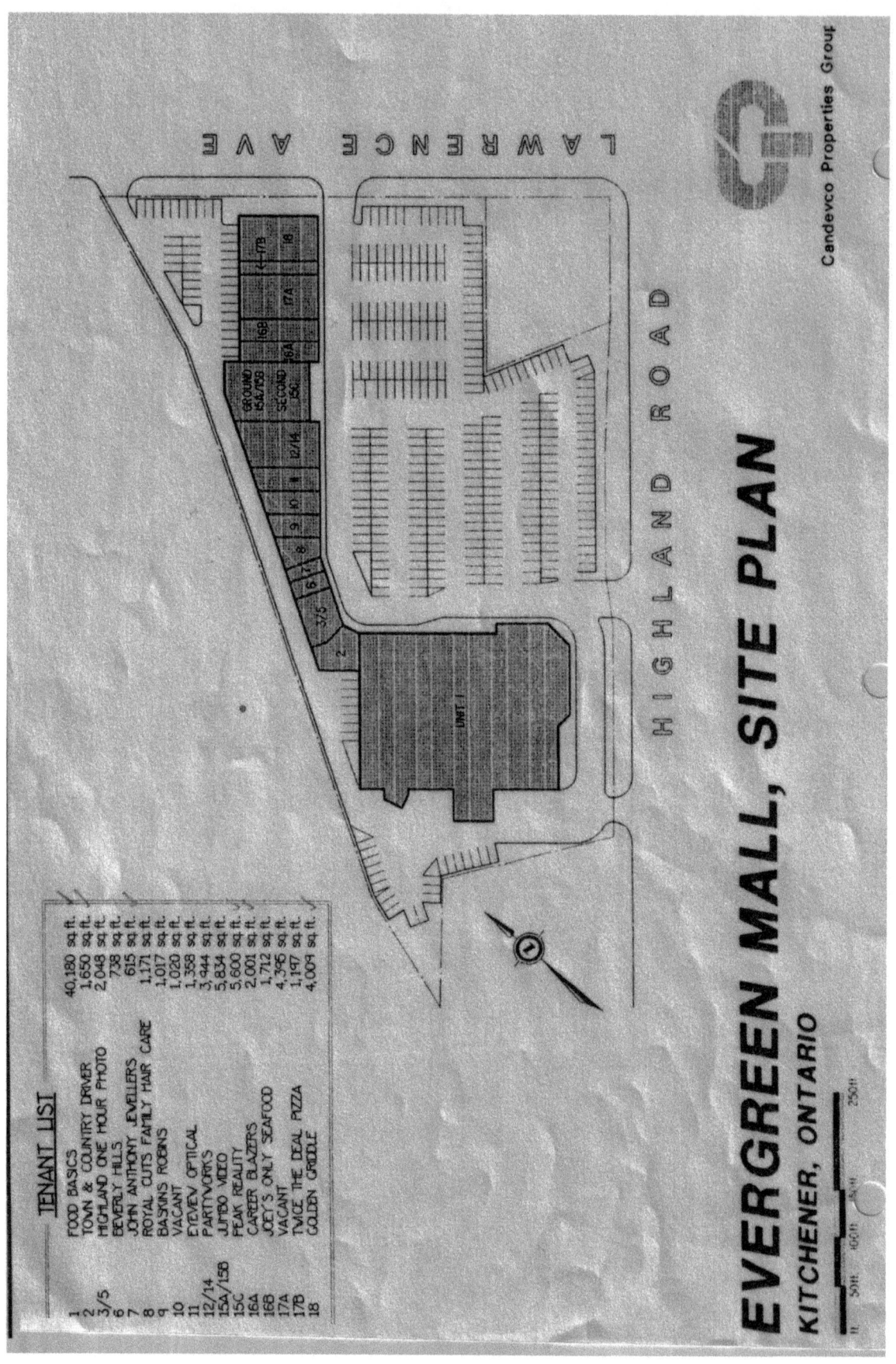

After all these years—CAN YOU BELIEVE IT—I was crushed by the action of local homeowners who had collected dozens of signatures (many from far away), opposing the development. It was at this time I learned about the contingencies of the Ontario Municipal Board—and the long, costly process needed to win its eventual and final approval.

Ariss Construction (Earl Riley) was contracted to build the project and all was going well until financing costs suddenly rocketed up to 18% and caused a panic. My bank manager called with questions, but I survived. In the end, the A & P store opened with drums and whistles —and guess who were first in line—some of those residents who earlier had objected!

I was proud of the attractive design and, by naming it Bullfrog Mall, recorded its historical connection to the early development of Guelph.

Note: A & P didn`t like the name 'Bullfrog' and used the street address in its advertising.

EVERGREEN MALL, KITCHENER, ABOUT 1980

Never at rest, I asked A & P managers about Kitchener and discovered that they had wanted a new grocery store there for some time, but finding a location was the problem. Working with Kenneth Fish, Project Manager, we hired a local planner to find us a suitable site. It took a long time and much direction from us, but eventually we chose a site at Highland Road and Lawrence, west of down-town King Street, Kitchener. There was a motel and pub on the street frontage and a large industrial truck repair business on the side street, but how to proceed? Try to buy them and get city approval or get approval first? We decided, with some hesitation, to first feel out the situation with the owners to measure their likely support or opposition, should we go ahead. Encouraged by A & P`s interest and unexpected endorsement by the local politician, we prepared a building plan to

Barry Scutt

"...purchase, close and move a big truck engine repair shop and sheds, and satisfy the owner who, first contact, had told me to get lost."

Barry Scutt

"The first excavations brought up a tangle of old cars and a mound of smelly earth...."

test the approval of a zone change with the city. We were asking for provisional approval of commercial zoning for a 100,000 sq ft shopping center. As usual, it required a huge effort of time, but we persisted until all the frustrating talk of zoning and competition studies was over. We thankfully moved on to the city council level, and it was arranged for us to meet with a council member—appointed to negotiate certain conditions to be met before final approval. We had to agree to relocate a major sanitary sewer, concrete the lining of the open water course at the rear of our property and cough up $100,000 cash for a narrow strip of parkland and fund a public trail at the rear of the property.

The big decision? We didn't own the land, so we had to close that busy, Evergreen Motel. We also had to buy and move that big truck engine repair shop and sheds, and satisfy the owner who, on first contact, had told me to get lost! (I felt it! Secretly, my gut feeling by this time was that both parties were ready for a change.)

So, with the valuable A & P lease to secure bank financing, I accepted the city proposal and applied great patience with skilled and experienced negotiations. Ken Fish and I, working together, were able to negotiate a buy-out of both landowners and put the project out for demolition of the buildings and call for construction bids.

We were present on site when that big backhoe moved into position to start work. After all the hard work to get there, what could go wrong? Well, we soon found out. SHOCK!

The first excavations brought up a tangle of old car bodies and a mound of smelly earth from an earlier gas station, which obviously had been dumped and buried there before being paved over for the motel parking lot (you never know!). It was of great concern at the time and called for the usual array of inspectors and experts and dump trucks, but fortunately, and with much relief, the contamination was limited to one area and work on excavation was restarted.

Construction went on for about six months under supervision of our site manager, freeing us to begin scouting for tenants to occupy the

40,000 sq ft of small stores that we knew, from experience, would make up and provide a balance of uses that make up a viable local shopping center. A big sign encouraging inquiries was erected on site and soon brought responses.

It took a year to get the Mall established as a successful local service center. We helped create a natural area and a footpath for local residents and, for the City of Kitchener—increased assessment.

To the reader, I hope you were interested and enjoyed reading these highlights selected from memory.

CLAIRFIELDS

A DEVELOPERS JOURNEY
By Philip Gosling AACI

CLAIRFIELDS – A DEVELOPER'S JOURNEY

Fifty years ago, I bought a farm in Puslinch (south of Guelph).

I met the owner in his stone house. He was married to the former owner's daughter, and not born to the farmer's life, he was a willing seller. I can still picture the farm lane—reaching half a mile from Gordon Street to the farmhouse—bales of straw, long forgotten, rotting in the fields, which tell a sad story. I paid $2,000 per acre for 90 acres on terms satisfactory to the owner and arranged a mortgage to be paid back over a long term.

It was out in the country, but I could see the future and was prepared to work and WAIT! I was also excited to be a farmer.

Each spring I was out there on the land. "I ploughed the fields and scattered the good seed." Starting with an old John Deere tractor and 3 furrow plough, the first year it took me 7 days to do it from dawn to dusk. I was in harmony with the moment. I was happy to be outdoors, planting and harvesting an annual crop of corn or grain that I would sell for a small profit to help pay the annual mortgage interest.

The farmhouse had its own history. My wife and I tried sleeping there, but snow mobiles, racing over fields and through the woodlot each night, drove us away, so for a few years I rented. First, I rented to an American couple escaping the Vietnam War draft and then to a newly married couple who started a garden and didn't seem to notice other people. I remember I dug a pond at the rear of the house that was soon home to a nesting pair of Canadian Geese. They had baby goslings, and I wrote to my mother in the United Kingdom, "We have added to our family." She wrote back that she was delighted by the news, only to be disappointed when I was forced to tell her that they were Canadian Geese goslings.

The large barn, built to store hay for animals in winter, led to a shocking discovery of solid layers of dried manure and bones. I offered the barn free to a Mennonite family who, on inspection, declined the offer, saying it was built of timber of mixed variety from the local woodlot and not of any value. The barn was eventually burned down. I can still see the flames!

I happily waited, until the growing City of Guelph annexed part of Puslinch Township, and it was time to start planning a future subdivision.

The first step was to acquire the large lot between my property and Clair Road. I had searched the title and there were two owners. This is when the real troubles began.

While looking for a partner with the all-important cash to offer the first owner, I entered an agreement with a well-known business friend who seemed to be very interested. Working together began with great promise, but then the unequal contribution of time and effort caused a rift and suddenly, without prior notice, my 'friend' exercised a buy-out clause in the agreement, forcing me to buy HIM out at an inflated price. It was a very costly learning experience.

The next exploit with lawyers marked the arrival of a gentleman I will not name, who attached himself to the Clair family. Although there was a purchase agreement in place, signed by all parties, he brought in an out-of-town lawyer to dispute a clause in the agreement. He then deliberately dragged an appeal over three successive court appearances. Each judge, on each appearance, agreed to have me 'examined' and held over for the next court. Finally, as the pile of evidence grew, we had a judge who ordered a closing at a higher price. It took more than a year of costly legal time and was a lesson on how lawyers can manipulate the legal system.

So now the subdivision process began. I handed a draft plan to Fred Woods, then City Manager. (It is worth noting that there were no municipal services available in the south end of Guelph at that time.)

"For those that think land development is easy AND have 13 years to spare," I summarize as follows. There were 10 STEPS that lay ahead.
READ ON:

ENGINEERING, STREET DESIGN, STREET NAMES, NDP ELECTION, ARCHELOGICAL SURVEY, SCHOOLING OBSTRUCTION, POSSIBLE CITY DUMP SITE, SANITARY SEWER TO GORDON STREET, PROPERTY SALE and BANK DEBT.

ENGINEERING

The site would require planning for a 100-year storm, which would include a 200-meter-wide floodway through the center of the subdivision (now the Gosling Gardens Park) and the sinking of a series of underground tanks designed to slow and store the water flow in the event of a storm. I will not go into the time lost when the Toronto consulting engineers, hired by the City of Guelph, and the engineers in Guelph, who we hired, disagreed over the design and cost of the floodway. There was an added requirement for 2 feet of matching subsoil to be spread over the north half of the land to ensure proper drainage to the floodway.

Then came the planners, who wanted a new STREET DESIGN to provide smaller lots and different STREET NAMES. I wanted street names that reflected my outdoor interests, but they got lost in favor of Guelph veterans' names. Also, my idea of living fences was abandoned, but there was one small area behind the original farmhouse that I held back! I named it Coopers Court! There were several reasons why. In my early farm wandering, I had located the nest of a 'Cooper's Hawk', (this is the hawk that catches birds, which is familiar to many homeowners with bird feeders). It is our usual winter visitor of note, and my street design could help protect its natural habitat. A 'COOPER' makes beer barrels (I owned Wellington Brewery at that time) and, because it was important to me, I named the street, Jean Anderson Crescent, in memory of my former wife, whose support was invaluable in those very busy early years.

Next, a major setback! THE ELECTION OF AN NDP GOVERNMENT! Bob Rae, Ontario Premier, changed all the planning rules overnight. New environmental studies were now required, affecting all local landowners. It caused an uproar! What could come next—I soon found out. An ARCHAEOLOGICAL SURVEY was ordered. A crew walked the site for days finding bits of crockery and glassware (coke bottles) marking places where first settlers once lived and, no less, an arrowhead! The search went on for 3 days, each day until nightfall, and to keep them from leaving early we erected and heated a tent (another cost). I asked what would happen to the bags of items collected and was told they would likely be 'stored in a basement'.

Then...guess what...the city was considering a new CITY DUMP SITE across from us on Clair Road and then we heard from the Guelph SCHOOL BOARD that, if we got approval, they would require us to pay the full cost of transporting the kids to the nearest school of choice!

Well, it had to end someday—a new government and Bob Rae was gone. The subdivision was finally approved (after 13 years of energetic struggle) and the time had come to build that necessary SANITARY SEWER from the industrial land on our west, under Hanlon Creek and dig a 40 ft deep trench through a drumlin (hill). It was designed —not just to service our lots, but to maintain gravity flow for sewage from new developments, which were now being planned, across from us—east and north of Gordon Street.

Was I prepared to oversee this? NO! I was weary, and by this time I had been thinking about making a change from land development to my growing interest in natural areas and land conservation.

I SOLD at a fair price, which enabled me to clear my BANK DEBT and have some extra. The new owners would prosper and enjoy the future—of this I was certain.

I closed the file and left. I was later amazed and pleased that (without prior knowledge) I was privileged to have my name given to the new GOSLING GARDENS ROAD and the GOSLING GARDENS PARK that connected with a trail to the Hanlon Creek Conservation Park and COOPERS COURT and JEAN ANDERSON CRESCENT.

FINAL RECOGNITION

It is of great importance that through all the years of planning and working together, I recognize the invaluable assistance of Kenneth Fish, Project Manager, and Lucy Fish, Office and Accountant Manager.

Note: The use of "I", mostly means 'WE' in all cases.

WELLINGTON COUNTY BREWERY
1980-95

Opening night at the local
Charles McLean, Dr. David Moorsom and Philip enjoying Real Ale at The Wooly in Guelph.

Early promotional flyer from the Duke of Grafton

Formally the Duke of Grafton

Charles MacLean...The Godfather of Ontario Craft Brewing

WELLINGTON COUNTY BREWERY

My Dad loved his beer. My first childhood memory is of waiting for him to have his pint or two at the local Yardley Arms pub on our way home (after moving furniture all day). At age 13 years I saw him and his pals chugging away at their twenty ounce pints at the public bar, but little else about pub life really registered (except warnings from my Mother), until I enlisted in the army, and went to a pub with the lads—and for the first time tasted the horrible stuff.

Time passed and the day came when at age 27, after 6 years of army service, some schooling, and tired of job searching, I left England for Canada...following in the footsteps of my father, and my brother, (about 30 years later). Once in Canada, I adapted quickly to the business climate and, liking it, was open to new ventures and in time, by chance...brewing beer.

It happened this way. I was returning to Guelph, after doing some business in Toronto, and feeling thirsty, decided to call in at the local Duke of Grafton pub (now the Shakespeare Arms). As I entered the pub I caught a waft of smoke of Erinmore Flake tobacco—an old favorite. There was a seat open next to the pipe smoker, and this is when I first met Charles McLean. I asked if I could join him and soon we were engaged in beer talk. He had this vision of brewing traditional English-style beer " REAL ALE and said he was looking for investors! (At the time I didn`t know Charles was credited with being the first to introduce 'Craft' beer to Ontario.)...Well, it didn't take long before I sampled his home brew, loved it and met with several potential investors. I heard them talk about importing a small brewery plant from England (no small plant being available in Canada or the U.S.). When a trip to U.K. was planned, I couldn't say NO and went along.

In London, we visited a small 10 barrel (360 gallons) brewery (located under a viaduct near the Thames River). What a thrill it was, the aroma was wonderful...imagine ...just being there. We observed the

Wellington Brewery on Woodlawn Road, Guelph

Oust house in England

brewing process, tasted the beer and I decided on the spot to join with the others—to help buy a similar plant and have it shipped to Guelph. Needless to say we celebrated our decision at several nearby pubs (I have a clouded memory of overlooking a yacht harbour) before returning home to Canada.

It was an exciting time for us, but by now there were serious decisions waiting to be made. To go ahead the Bank needed extra security from the investors. The small investors chose not to continue, leaving two principal owners: Dr. David Moorsom, (D.M.), a busy, highly respected medical doctor in Toronto, and me, a local Land Developer and, as it turned out, a 'client' of the same Bank as the brewery, so you can see how my Path was slowly being decided for me.

Regarding premises for the brewery, after a search for a suitable site failed, I recommended the purchase of City-owned frontage on Highway 7 (a good move I thought) also to find a suitable builder of the plant. We had brought back some plans and ideas from UK, but we needed a lot of engineering help with the interior site plan. The exterior design, with some imagination, we settled on the look of an Oasthouse (in U.K...used for drying hops). I also added a pub which I called the IRON DUKE HOUSE.

Well, it was a long wait, but finally our new brewery arrived and was delivered to our new building on Highway #7. We had hired an engineer to oversee the construction of the building and also locate the brew-house and processing tanks. Regarding the exterior look from the highway, I wanted an exterior design to like an English Oasthouse with a small garden up front .

 It was an exciting time and we hurried to commission the plant so we could sample the first brew. For us it was magical, and not knowing its strength, we got nicely err...pissed!

.....LIFE WAS GOOD ! Now all we had to do was sell the beer and make lots of money..... but no thought had been given to sales, marketing or

"We needed to teach the servers how to keep the ale fresh in the casks."

...not square containers but round ones like soccer balls.

One litre plastic bottles

Gosling family enjoying a 'Welly'

distribution…or that we needed a license to brew and sell beer…(it's the alcohol you know…needs to be regulated!). We quickly realized experienced help was needed to manage the brewing process. Dr M, on a visit to London, hired a qualified Master Brewer. I rented a home for him and his wife and kids in Guelph…but he didn't stay long! He left for Labbatt's, after one year, but thankfully he did train a University of Guelph grad as his successor. You know, I remember being OK with this, as his idea of working hours did not match with the 24/7 time commitment expected by a business guy (like me) in Canada. Meanwhile, Dr M, who was well known in Toronto, along with other aspiring brewers, helped persuade the Ontario Government to change the rules for small brewers. He also applied his negotiating skills to gain access to the Beer Stores and LLBO. So it was a struggle, it took time, but eventually we were on our way.

The news of Ontario's first microbrewery travelled fast, and our offer to install pumps to 'pull a pint' of REAL ALE at pubs, was widely publicized…the publicity was wonderful, except we soon found there was a problem. We needed to teach the servers how to keep the ale fresh in `'asks', (cellarman skills). That ultimately, and regrettably at the time, caused us to change our plans.

On the packaging side, since we had no bottling line, we started hand filling one gallon plastic containers and delivering them to beer stores. What fun!, It turned out that yeast in the unfiltered beer (Real Ale) while in the containers, continued to ferment, and the result, after being shaken up in delivery, was not square containers but round ones, like soccer balls, that proved 'just a little' difficult to stack at beer stores! (They loved us). So we switched to a 2 litre and then 1 litre plastic bottles, until finally we acquired some mechanical help and obtained glass bottles from Brewers Retail, who then consented to sell our beer in the Beer Stores, which helped us survive the early years.

"Yeah," I often said, "brewing good beer was the easy part—selling it- was the real problem."

My old regiment,"The Coldstream Guards" visited Kitchener.

Good time was had by all after the bands played and marched.

Lets face it! Change happens.

Dr David Moorsom advised me that he was relocating and not able to continue his investment in Wellington, so I decided…well…just 'do it'—and I set out to promote beer sales by myself…you know, it was fun visiting pubs—I bought a lot of pints, drank gallons of Real Ale (at the local 'Wooly Pub') and tried with little success, at first, to sell draft beer in kegs for delivery in Toronto. But it was tiring, and after 10 plus years of effort and personal financial support, along with the business now growing, it was time for me to make a proposal to the young brewers…I was ready.

BUT…there were special events of note I want to remember.

I learned that the military band of my old regiment, the Coldstream Guards was on tour in the United States and Canada, and would visit Kitchener on a certain date in September.

Well, business aside, I was delighted and quickly made arrangement for a bar to be set up with 'casks' of Real Ale in a large dining room in the Kitchener Arena. And when the marching and musical performances ended, invited upstairs, we pulled pints of beer from hand pumps for the men (like they would know from England.) I had brought in pint glasses, and we all raised them with customary salutes (CHEERS)…as we sat around. I was thrilled with their presence and made a short speech as a former Guardsman #2671062, that was loudly cheered. Later I was introduced to the packed house in the arena where the bands played and marched. It was an amazing experience I shall never forget.

But there is more.

Two weeks before the event, I was told there would be an advance party visit by a Sargeant of the Coldstream Guards and a Piper from the Queens Own Highlanders. (It proved to be a combined event). On arrival, I invited them to stay at my home overnight, where they quickly found my scotch. At about 6 pm I drove them down to my local pub 'the Wooly', where they stood at the bar in uniform. I was

Doug Hawkins (left) and Michael Stirrup, vice president and president respectively of Wellington Brewery, stand behind the bar in the Iron Duke House the hospitality room for visitors to the brewery.

Philip Gosling, Founder of Wellington Brewery (back), with co-owners of the Woolwich Arms, Jean-Pierre Schoch (left) and Bob Desautels (right) in 1993

The 'Wooly' Guelph

The Feathers Pub...Toronto

very proud, and then, at my request, the piper retrieved his bagpipes from my car and to the disbelief of those gathered around him, played the haunting notes of DESERT STORM, which he had written while in Iraq.

Well, it was all together a great success. And the promotors asked me to do the same for the next year. I said NO...they were bringing a different regiment.

Another event was setting up a bar for Wellington beer at a Jazz Concert in Toronto. It was a difficult job, carrying kegs and beer up two floors and not encouraging when a guy comes up and asks for a Labatt's Blue? The Jazz was great and when over, the band leader asked me up to the stage to meet the musician who played the trombone, he said "His name is John Gosling," and for fun I replied "Great, you know I always wanted to play a trombone." John's reply was that he would teach me to play for shares in the brewery.

Well, my 13 years at 'Wellington' sadly came to an end when my wife, Jean, was diagnosed with lung cancer. She was quite ill, and I drove her to the General Hospital in Hamilton three times a week for radiation treatments. The doctors were very kind to her but the prognosis was bad, and I knew it was the right time to offer the assets of the brewery to the young and ambitious top brewers with an opportunity to take over the brewery business. I would offer to sell them the land and building later...if they prospered (WHICH THEY DID). So, now free of the responsibility, I was able to give full time to my real estate business and follow another PATH.

I was pleased and proud to have helped start a new, successful business for Guelph.

Note: Wellington County Brewery, as it was first named, was the first micro-brewery in Ontario. The first Real Ales brewed were Original County Ale and Arkell Best Bitter. Our first pubs were the Wooly, in Guelph, and Feathers, in Toronto.

The Duke of Wellington was born May 1769, died Sept 1852. His actual name was Arthur Wellesley. He had a brilliant military career which included defeating Nepolean in the Battle of Waterloo in 1815. He was Prime Minister twice after his military career, once in 1828 then again briefly in 1834. During his time in office he legislated the public house (pub) to encourage people to drink beer rather than gin. His troops called him The Iron Duke because of the way he disciplined them.

REAL ALE

Wellington Brewery is the first brewery to in Canada dedicated to the commercial production of traditional English style Real Ale.

The main benefit to the consumer is that Real Ale delivers a fresher, full bodied taste.

Real Ale is define as casked-conditioned beer brewed according to the strictest, centuries old British brewing tradition.

Cask conditioning is the natural aging process that preserves all the natural flavour and natural carbonation of the brew.

Real Ale is unfiltered, unpasteurized and free of additives and preservatives

Real Ale is served at cellar temperature, about 12 degrees C (55F)

All of these factors allow the full, natural flavour of the beer to come through.

Part Two
THE MISSION

NATURE
Protect and Preserve

OUTDOOR ART & SCIENCE SCHOOL
— a charitable non-profit organization —
Registered #0516856-20-15

BOARD OF DIRECTORS
Philip R. Gosling
Dr. Owen V. Washburn
Dr. Robert G. C. MacLaren
Raymond N. Lowes
Norman Pearson

Mailing Address
P.O. Box 112
Guelph, Ont. N1H 6J6
Administrative Office
375 Edinburgh Rd. S.
Guelph, Ont. N1E 2K7
822-4062

NATURE — "PROTECT AND PRESERVE"

The PATH I found and followed

From early childhood my greatest happiness came from time spent out-of-doors, walking a country path to school, looking for bird nests, catching frogs, or climbing trees. It was when my roots were firmly planted 'in the good earth' that nourished a love of nature and gave me direction and courage to pursue my hopes and dreams.

I pick up my tale here.

In 1956, I was driving my car on business and, half listening to the CBC radio, heard a 'preacher's' voice refer to a two-week nature camp at the Billie Bear Lodge in Muskoka. At this camp, I heard, "Retired university professors lead walks and give talks on the science and wonders of nature." At first his words passed by me, but then, suddenly stirred by an inner yearning for change and a rest, I felt drawn to go to this camp. It was a future PATH; it was meant for me. I signed up.

The Camp experience went like this....

We were walking quietly on a forest path when, hushed to silence, I felt a tap on my shoulder, then another tap. "Can you hear it now?" asked the retired professor behind me (I'm a little deaf). "It's a tiny bird singing just above us—a blue winged warbler," he said. He told me how this little bird had flown over 2,000 miles from South America to raise a family in our northern forest. I was immediately 'smitten' with love for this tiny bird. Then I heard of the miracle of bird migration, where millions of birds, small and large, return each year to nest and raise families in Canada—to the place they called Home.

So inspired, I had to learn more. After those two weeks of study, fun, and discovery, I returned home to Guelph, eager to pass on my new-found knowledge to anyone prepared to listen, including my golf partners—(while playing)—a habit I never lost (ask them!).

I joined the local naturalist club and soon paid a visit to the University of Guelph's Arboretum to look for birds and native trees. Getting more involved, I offered support for a Wildlife Garden being designed, and later funded the Outdoor Art and Science School, established to present courses to young and older students on natural history and the environment.

This was the beginning of change in my future goals.

In the ensuing thirty busy and productive years—although always insightful of development opportunities—I never lost my instinct for protecting nature and the desire to further my education in conservation and nature reserves and how I could get more involved.

As a Bruce Trail Founder and trail director, I had observed the energy lying latent in volunteers eager to commit to building "The Trail" to protect the natural beauty of the Niagara Escarpment. I wondered how I might direct that same energy to long-term ideas for permanent investment in the future. I decided on leaving a lasting legacy by founding THE GOSLING FOUNDATION.

OLD FRIENDS
Philip Gosling, Bob Bateman and Bob Taylor.

The Bruce Trail
STORIES   Philip Gosling CM

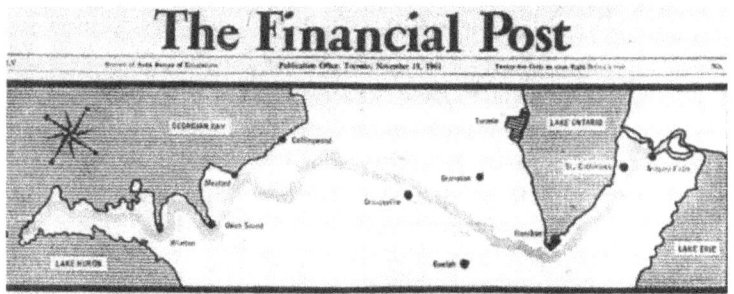
Press release November 18 1961

Signing of the B.T.A. incorporation Papers 1963

Kitchener- Waterloo Record January 26, 1962

Measuring the Trail

"....parked my car, donned my binoculars and began walking"

Philip painting first blaze

Philip with Doug Brown celebrating the Gosling side trail and first blaze

Where it all began...

MY BRUCE TRAIL STORY

"A naturalists Dream. A Miracle of Volunteerism. Protected FOREVER"

MAY 14th 1962

It is my first day as Bruce Trail Director.

I had planned for this. I headed south from Guelph to the underpass of Highway 401 near Kelso, parked my car, 'donned' my binoculars and began walking. There was a little house nearby. I knocked the front door and made my first speech about building a trail to Tobermory. The homeowner, unsure of where I had sprung from, and evidently not impressed, told me, "Come back if a trail ever gets built."

I set out to prove him wrong.

Continuing my walk, I climbed over a fence just up the road and headed north through heavy bush, over and around rocks, fallen trees and tree stumps and stopped. Gravel pit ahead! I turned back. I had learned enough by then to know what challenges lay ahead. I wrote to Founder Ray Lowes, "I`ve started—only 300 miles to go!"

So here I am now, 60 years later (it's hard to believe), feeling excited at the prospect of telling short stories (vignettes), with fun, matching graphics, of some remarkable people and events I met or experienced in my first years as Bruce Trail Director. I will include a few bits of history to add interest and make some observations of nature that I remember from those early days...and maybe you will share a smile or two with me, at my British sense of humor.

NIAGARA 'BRUCE TRAIL CLUB'

I remember meeting Bert Lowe in the fall. An early starter he and his naturalist friends had already marked a trail from Queenston

Short Hills Nature Reserve

Ray Lowes at southern Cairn of Bruce Trail

" In spring it is possible to see waves of our northern hawks migrating north"

Tulip trees in flower

(now the site of the southern cairn)and headed north under and over major highways—an amazing feat which they then proudly named The Niagara Escarpment Trail—with yellow blazes! I thanked him for doing my job, but then he had given me a new job...to convince him to join the Bruce Trail Association and change the blazes from yellow to white!

Bert was fun to talk to. He was a keen birder and naturalist who could name birds and most plants and trees—err...are you a tree lover? On a last walk (survey) with Bert through Short Hills Provincial Park, I picked up some seeds of a giant Tulip Tree (collecting seeds is a habit of mine) which at home later, found in my pocket, I thumbed into a pot of daffodil bulbs sitting on a window ledge. To my surprise—some months later—the seeds germinated and when grown about 10 inches high, I first potted, and then planted the seedlings in my garden. Today, I am proud of the two giant 60 ft high tulip trees I greet every day—host to birds and butterflies—a living symbol for me of the Bruce Trail and its beginning—to be protected FOREVER.

I headed north now through famous Niagara wine country—past the lovely Balls Falls Conservation Park (a lovely spot to visit) and on towards Grimsby. There is a high peak there! It is known by birdwatchers as Beamer Point (or Hawk Cliffs). In the spring, it is the place to watch waves of hawks migrating north to their breeding grounds. You can mingle here with experts—all with binoculars searching the skies, who can rapidly identify species by their size, wing shape, and flight patterns—gliding, diving or direct flight—an exciting challenge for birdwatchers, young and old.

HAMILTON

Where the Founders first 'dreamed' of a trail along the Niagara Escarpment and when the idea hit the news, Hamilton residents,

THE FOUNDERS

L to R Dr. Bert McLaren, Ray Lowes, Philip Gosling, Norman Pearson

excited by the prospect of building a public trail, came from all areas to help weave a trail through parks, subdivisions and public places: Dundas, Hamilton, Burlington and back to Highway 401 (where I started months earlier).

It was a momentous time and a revelation to see how different groups, some wanting independence at first, came together as one community and with the four Founders present, celebrated the private initiative and community spirit in the building of their section of "THE BRUCE TRAIL', destined to be open and free to the public for future generations to enjoy "FOREVER".

For excellent details, read *Iroquoia Bruce Trail Club Memoirs* by Ian Reid. April, 2000.

TORONTO

The FIRST public gathering of the Bruce Trail was June 28, 1962. About 30 invitations had gone out to newspapers, nature, and hiking clubs, and to Ray Lowes many correspondents. I had booked a room for 50 persons at Edwards Gardens in Toronto, and waited—100 showed up! I was blown over at this huge response. "Help build a trail for hiking along the Niagara Escarpment." A newspaper man asked, "Can they save that ribbon of wilderness?"

Like an evangelist, I called for followers: "Let's do it!"

Volunteers lined up and, eager to make a start, a first survey/hike was arranged for the following weekend.

Seven of us met, somewhere close to Georgetown, climbed a fence and crossed an open field. (Oh! that childhood nightmare of being chased by wild horses.) Two hikers on that first Toronto hike, Jim Allan and Doug Brown, became special friends. You know, looking back, I remember being so moved at having them, and so many others

Left to right...Ian Lamont-Smith, Doug Brown, Diedre Clark, Harold Wills, Philip Gosling, Douglas Campbell, Jim Allen

"Seven of us met, somewhere close to Georgetown, climbed a fence and crossed an open field"

"...he asked me if he could spend a night in a sleeping bag on my front lawn to gain experience..."

John Robarts, Ontario Premier 1961-1971

like them, offering to help and give their time freely to support the Founders' mission.

Jim Allan was different and it's why I liked him! One day, doing an audit on a winter visit to Guelph, he asked me if he could spend a night in a sleeping bag on my front lawn, "to gain experience," he said. (His wife had said to him, "Not on my front lawn, you don't!") He scooped a hollow in the snow, slept in his sleeping bag, made his own tea from 'melted snow' (I watched him, through a partly drawn curtain) which he boiled on his tiny primus stove, then packed up, got dressed back in his car and, after waving to the worried lady next door (gave her a thumb up), went off to his work, declining to come indoors.

Another time, I visited Jim at the Terra Cotta Conservation Area (a Bruce Trail camp site) and was really surprised to find him in a homemade 'TEEPEE'. He invited me to come inside, and I met his wife and giggling children. They were amused at me watching smoke from an inside fire curl up to an opening to the sky.

THEN a great surprise—an official looking letter arrived on March 20th, 1963.

I was invited to visit with Ontario Premier John Robarts at Queen's Park in Toronto. I am not sure how this came about. Ray Lowes and Norman Pearson were both active addressing groups like the Conservation Council of Ontario and the Ontario Naturalists (now Ontario Nature and the original sponsor of The Bruce Trail) but I guess as Trail Director, I was out there—the front man—in the field 'raising an army'. Anyway, Premier Robarts greeted me warmly and asked how did this trail idea get started?

I explained the four Founders were naturalists and, for a project, elected to see that the Niagara Escarpment be better protected. "It is a wonderful natural resource not being recognized," I declared, "and the idea of building a hiking trail along its length is gaining much needed public attention"—my voice now raised for effect—(as were

Scottish Wish that worked for us despite the smoke from the new fireplace...

Ian Reid, Barbara Reid and Philip

Tom East, Mimi and Bill Hamilton with Philip

Philip and Susan Gosling

Philip and Dave Tyson

Celebrating the first blaze

his eyebrows.) Mindful of politics, I then spoke of how hundreds of volunteers were now forming clubs to build and blaze the trail from Niagara to Tobermory, and generous landowners were allowing free access to their properties. I could see he was impressed and, turning to a senior staff member, he suggested, "We need a 3–5-year plan." I stood up, thanked him for the invitation and left, believing, and hoping that one day, the Bruce Trail Founders and all Bruce Trailers Builders would be remembered for their commitment and action. "Can they save this ribbon of wilderness?"

CALEDON

It was the first gathering of the 'CALEDON BRUCE TRAIL CLUB' at my home in Guelph. After a big WELCOME to those present (some had come from a distance) I remember lighting a fire in my newly 'rebuilt' fireplace in the living room and, with due ceremony, offering the Scottish wish "lang may yer lum reek" that promises a long life and a happy future—but disaster! A choking cloud of smoke from a 'un-rebuilt' chimney, engulfed the room and drove us outside—coughing and laughing—yet did not diminish our dream for the future.

Surveying the escarpment for the best route was a challenge. One day at Credit Falls, I decided to go out on my own and got lost, and also lost my car. A little worried, I knocked on a door in the village and 'with cap in hand' asked the hesitant lady who answered, would she mind helping me find my car? Well, it didn't take long to find it and I was able to thank her for her kindness and TRUST! She replied, "You we're lucky—I would not have helped, had it not been for seeing binoculars around your neck!"

Referring again to Credit Falls, Tom East and I were trying to find a way for the trail to descend down the escarpment from a high point

"...she would not have helped had it not been for seeing the binoculars around my neck."

"....I pulled over and was forced to watch the following cars speed by."

(L to R) Dave Platt (Past President).
Philip Gosling, Beth Kummling (Executive Director),
Tristan Kummling, Janice McClelland (President)

(we had not got a welcome from the resident landowners) so, aided by a compass bearing, we followed a historic road allowance through trees and bush and by absolute luck found a break in the cliff face (it's a tough climb there down, or up). Now known as the 'Devils Pulpit' (not sure who named it), there is a plaque there—please note the special people in the photo. Just for the memory, it is where nearby, on bended knee, I proposed to Jean, my assistant, who remains very much part of my personal early Bruce Trail history.

A local Rotarian Club member once asked if I would lead a tour to the Bruce Trail. "Sure," I said, and some weeks later I was leading a convoy of a dozen cars near Orangeville when (OMG) my car ran out of gas. I pulled over and was forced to watch the following cars speed by, only to get lost—near Hockley Valley—I was told. Much embarrassed, I met up with some of the drivers later at the local pub and offered to buy a round, and I can say... it cost me a lot more than a tank full of gas!

Often, when talking to volunteers, many older and more experienced than myself, I was told that I spoke to them like a Sgt Major (OK men/people, line-up—this is what we are going to do! Yes, if I think of it now, it was true (I still speak like that—ASK MY WIFE!), but I had committed to 'put the trail on the ground' in one year and that is what I was gonna do!

SHELBURNE

I was greeted warmly at the home of Grant and Grace Bell. At first hesitant to get involved, they later agreed to find volunteers for the Highland Bruce Trail Club to mark a trail through this highest and most beautiful part of Ontario. A well-respected writer, Fred Bosworth described his experience of the trail at this high point for an article in McLean's Magazine and later published in *Readers' Digest* in 1970.

"....others told me I was too bossy and maybe I still am (ask my wife)"

"One day Grant Bell accused me of ruining his retirement"

Walter and Edna Blacklot

Article in Readers Digest (April 1968) by Fred Bosworth.

Grant Bell, who later became a valuable member of the Bruce Trail Conservancy Board, 'with fingers wagging,' accused me of ruining his plans for a quiet retirement.

COLLINGWOOD

The City Hall in Collingwood was the only place I could find to host the potential members of the 'BLUE MOUNTAIN CLUB'. I met with George Willis, a friendly man interested and learned in local history. He helped me contact about a dozen or so locals who were invited to attend a meeting to start a trail club. After my now 'practiced and rousing talk', one man, Walter Blacklock, took me aside and in his northern English accent told me he was not a 'joiner' but would blaze a trail with his wife and others above the Blue Mountain ski-hills and be gone! And that is exactly what happened—a huge distance. Then I heard that he had he left his job at the local hospital and retired to Scotland. I never met or spoke to him again, which I most regret, but his astonishing contribution lives on.

Always, watching birds—there was one special bird I spotted—a peregrine falcon (the world`s fastest bird in flight) over the elevators in Collingwood. You know, I covered many miles, driving from one club to another often with eyes everywhere except on the road. I was bad—really bad on some days. Yeah!—fortunate—and lucky?

For interest, in my final report to the F.O.N., my helper, Jean, reported I had driven 23,000 miles to and from the escarpment in 1962-1963.

BEAVER VALLEY

This area is lovely and appealing, not just for its natural valley beauty and ski hills (I skied there a few times and one time got my car stuck

"....there was one special bird I spotted....a peregrine falcon."

"...and lost my rear bumper when it was pulled off....being rescued."

Thornbury Fishway

"...a family of racoons busily and noisily, eating the family left-overs"

in a snow drift and lost my rear bumper when it was pulled off—being rescued.

Thornbury, at the mouth of the Beaver River, is an attractive town, combining a river/lake frontage with a fishing opportunity. I remember visiting the river dam there in the spring to watch the spectacle of salmon leaping up a man-made ladder trying to reach their spawning grounds up-river. Go visit!

It was here at a meeting with Keith Soloman, 'BEAVER BRUCE TRAIL CLUB' leader, that I asked, "What is that noise?" (that no one seemed to notice.) We were deep into discussion on 'how to approach a landowner for permission to blaze a trail when, at a second loud noise the homeowner host stood up and opened an overhead door to show a family of raccoons busily and noisily eating the family leftovers while listening into our organizing details.

OWEN SOUND

I loved the town of Owen Sound, but boy, that snow! Driving on streets through downtown, the snowbanks were so high that children could not be seen walking to school, except in cut-outs at driveways.

I reserved a hall, in the library I think, and with help, I mailed out personal letters to about 30 early contacts who I thought would be interested—inviting them to attend a meeting. Boards were set up by Jean, showing a trail winding its way up the Bruce Peninsula to Tobermory. Wow! We were so excited by the attendance. From the start, most credit should go to the first volunteers, Charles Middlebro and John Stuart (who seemed to know everyone present) and agreed to lead the organizing that followed. Malcolm Kirk, a Bruce County conservation officer, was particularly helpful in guiding me around nature reserves and I remember him pointing out the 'walking fern' at Inglis Falls and, at another location, we

John Stewart

Charlie Middlebro

Mac Kirk

Walking Fern

"...we watched a male bluebird feeding young inside a hollowed out cedar post."

Wiarton Willy in summer?

watched a male blue bird feeding young inside a hollowed-out cedar post.

The first volunteers (later named the 'SYDENHAM BRUCE TRAIL CLUB') began trail work at a furious pace, and in less than 12 months from their start, on November 27, 1963, Charles Middlebro announced the completion of their 60-mile section of the trail from Beaver Valley to Wiarton. I remember the thrill and excitement felt by all the volunteer trail builders at work along the trail at that news.

Again, it was time for me to move on, but I must mention there are many outstanding sites for views over Georgian Bay that have since become favorite stops for hikers. Several local authors have written excellent books that I'll mention later.

WIARTON

The famous home of the groundhog that predicts the coming of spring offers wonderful access to visitors for fishing and sailing on Colpoy Bay. I recall greeting the first volunteers and feeling somewhat overcome by their commitment to build the trail down to the water's edge in town. All trail enthusiasts were invited to meet at the Arlington Hotel downtown (nice place to meet for lunch and a pint, and where I stayed overnight on my first visit). Word reached out to a local politician who helped contact some important landowners. It was here I met Ron Gatis, who I later described as a 'quiet, giant of a man'. I was so appreciative of him and his family. From the start, they made generous contributions, and provided leadership in support of the Bruce Trail Conservancy and in particular the 'PENINSULAR BRUCE TRAIL CLUB'. I regret not getting to know him better. I was always moving on.

Now I have two lasting and different memories to relate.

Ron Gatis

High Dump 300'
Log Chute

" I just kept going...blind...counting up one, two, three, four until the road was clear."

While still at Wiarton, and before I moved on, I was invited to join with a local group heading out for their annual deer hunting expedition—an experience quite new to me. With others I drove some miles north to where we left our cars off of Highway 6 and I clearly remember walking with others behind a wagon loaded with supplies and enough beer for a month, and 'drinking some' on the way to their secluded camp.

On the next two mornings, the hunters left camp for known spots where they could hide and wait—guns ready—I assumed. However, before leaving, on the first morning, I was given directions to a spot on the escarpment called 'High Dump', where in past times, harvested logs were sent down a chute 300 feet to barges waiting below. Hmm! It was not too far for me to walk there—through thick bush—but I admit to some hesitation when advised to wear a red hat and try not to behave like a deer, you know, with all those friendly hunters with guns out there?

The third morning, after giving my thanks and gratitude for the beer and fun, I walked out, following the path we had made on the way in, but now, on my own, singing, 'Oh Canada' and wearing my red toque, as advised.

The second memory—I was in a hurry and on my way south, I stopped for gas in Wiarton. While filling up, two car drivers approached me and asked if I intended to drive on, and if so, could they follow me (they were concerned about the weather.) "Sure," I said, and started up the hill with two cars following. Leaving the town limits, I was immediately hit with a blinding snowstorm 'white out'. I began counting—one, two, three, four (I could see the tops of telephone poles and kept going), but kept my eye on the rear mirror—NO FOLLOWERS? Later, on the same stretch of highway, drifts were really bad and in some places higher than my car, but at the time (I admit—I knew no better) I would drive on without stopping. That is what the weather was like in the sixties! Wouldn't do it today—you bet!

Moving on, I had arranged to visit the 'CAPE CROKER PARK RESERVE' to meet with trail volunteer John Nadjiwon and also to

Lion's Head

John Nadjiwon

Read about the Peninsular Club in Trail to the Bruce

attend a meeting with Chippewa Band Chief Vernon Jones. What an extraordinary experience that was for me! The band members were so supportive. (I wrote to Ray Lowes, who I kept advised of my progress, and he wanted me to plan a visit there for himself!)

Then it was on to a final gathering of Bruce Trail pioneers, but I feel remiss not mention two books of importance that will ever remain in my memory: *Bruce Beckons* by Dr Sherwood Fox (that speaks for itself) and *The Trail to the Bruce* by David Tyson (written with an excellent, personal commitment to detail).

At Lions Head, at the home of Reeve Elsie Graig, I was thrilled to meet Charles Middlebro, Ron Gatis, Alan Fowler, Jack Johnstone and other important volunteers I regret I can't remember. This was my last opportunity to thank them for their valuable support of the Bruce Trail. I gave an up-date of the amazing progress to date and of the many commitments made to safeguard the escarpment for future generations. It was a heart-warming and thrilling experience—just being there and able to meet and talk with these very important and experienced local leaders.

Closer to Tobermory, I called in at the lodge of Jack and Sheila Johnson—located 7 miles in from Highway 6! Jack, a farmer and politician, became an indispensable friend and supporter of the Trail. One day, I walked a few miles into the bush with Jack, and on a quiet moment he said to me how he loved to get away from it all. In the years that followed, Jack and Sheila hosted a party of young hikers from several countries, who, having completed the 'north end' of the trail, were celebrating receipt of the International 'Duke of Edinborough Award'.

Note: this was after my time as trail director, but it is worth telling that the Bruce Trail Founders met with and were praised by Prince Philip for their environmental vision when attending a Canadian Audubon event months earlier in Toronto.

Duke of Edinburgh's Award

"Lloyd Smith gave me a hand-made carving of a captains head..."

Alfie Adams

The trail, first envisioned, was to end at what I think is now called Trail End Lodge. In a much earlier time, it was a wireless station purposed to track and warn passing ships of the dangerous cliffs and rocks in bad weather. The station manager then, I was told, was known as a Mr. Gosling! Who told me this? My new friend Alfie.. read on…

Note: Tobermory was a lovely fishing village at the time. I was happy there and after a final visit to Flowerpot Island with Leo Smith, tour boat guide (I treasure the carving of a boat captain's head he gave me), I saw my commitment 'to put the trail on the ground' coming to an end.

Now, my most lasting memory remains of my time spent talking with Alfie in his small house near the northern Bruce Trail Cairn.

Note: The first minutes of the Peninsula Trail Club from 1964 lists Alfie Adams as chairman. I wrote this tribute based on a multitude of pleasant memories and written with the deepest of affection. The "others" to whom I refer in the last stanza are Jack Johnston, Alan Fowler, Charles Middlebro, John Stuart, Keith Soloman, Walter Blacklock, and others.

ODE TO ALFIE ADAMS

One plate, one fork on a table top
And a saucepan half full of cold stew
The plate would be washed just before the next meal
But everything else ... it'll do

Clothes on a nail on a door ... or the bed
Boots and an old rug on the floor.
The black stove and pot gave warmth to the room
And wood chips made a trail to the door.

On Alfie's head ... and tied in a knot
Was a strand of hair from each side.
When he came in from out back
He would take off his cap
Drawing eyes to the bald spot he would hide.

We sat and talked to the early hours
Alfie thrived on folk lore.
He spoke on the search for a sunken ship (The Griffon)
And mining of materials on shore.

We talked about his land and way of life
"You can't trust a lawyer," he said.
And he surveyed his own lines with a stake and his eye
And invested in whiskey instead.

In the winter, the wind would pile snow at his door
And he would dig a path to his shed
And his whiskey came in on the Greyhound bus
Which he hid in the wall by his bed

In summertime, he said wrens clamoured all day
And flowers grew wild in his yard
It was time to visit Cyprus Lake and the bush
He'd think about work ... but not hard

Alf helped build the trail in his own special way
And I learned about living alone
And of a simple life where no goals are set
Free to think, or to dream, or to roam

I am sad that Alfie and others
Are not with us today
Though their lives each so different, I believe,
Were I able to visit them in their homes today
I would be in no hurry to leave?

P. R. Gosling, September 14 1985

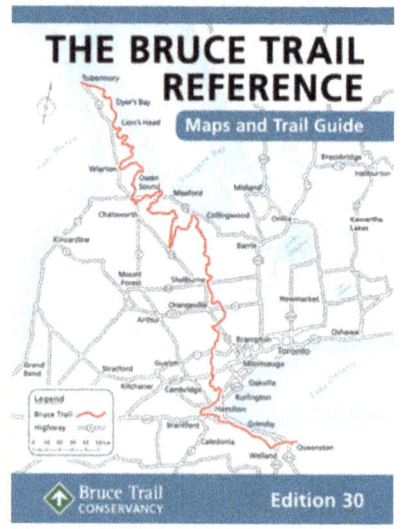

GOSLING FOUNDATION

Some of the many events sponsored by the Gosling Foundation

THE GOSLING FOUNDATION
by Stan Kozak, retired Executive Director

In my many conversations with Philip Gosling over the years he often reflected on a time when the stresses of a stellar real estate career loomed up and looked to overwhelm. A radio ad to attend Billy Bear Nature camp for adults run by the Federation of Naturalists reached out to him and he took it. On one of the camp outings a blue winged warbler sang from a tree top and through it nature touched a tired but amazed businessman.

Whether it was the astrological destiny of a Leo or simply the needs of an ego driven to achieve, the dye was cast. With the intertwining of business acumen and a fascination with nature, and a desire to give back, the Gosling Foundation was created.

Several big ideas or inspirations informed Philips' thoughts and actions influencing the work of the foundation:

- Cultivate the community of those with an interest in nature and near interests in nature.

- Make no small plans…

- Find the leaders with the ideas and ambitions and nurture them.

- Volunteers can turn the world around.

The Outdoor Art and Science School, initiated about 1978 was the first iteration of the foundation. It presented short courses in nature appreciation on topics such as bird identification, nature photography, whale conservation, wild like wood carving and natural landscaping in three communities, Guelph, Kitchener Waterloo and Brantford Ontario.

The school went on to prompt and support the Gosling Wildlife Gardens at the Arboretum, University of Guelph, as well as the Elm Recovery Project there, later greatly advanced by research at GRIPP. The Gosling Resarch Institute for Plant Preservation, at the University.

Land trusts involved in the acquisition of land ecological importance from British Columbia to Nova Scotia were supported in their work. A number of those received their start-up funding from the foundation.

In Ontario, promising areas were identified for the development and support such as the Nature Festival Seed Fund and the integrated four credit outdoor program operating in some secondary schools.

In 2014 the foundation partnered with the Sustainability Network to bring the knowledge and practice of engagement organizing to nature groups across Canada. Leading practitioners were brought in to conduct workshops and webinars and the transformation was begun. Learning was greatly enhanced through the creation of communities of practice where a half dozen or so nature organizations would learn together to put into practice the skills of engaging and mobilizing people power to appreciate and protect nature.

Every participating organization advanced on some level and some were transformed, the Couching Conservancy, Nature Trust of New Brunswick and Nature Canada to name a few. Nature Canada continues this work with it's greater than one thousand partnering organizations across the country.

The Gosling Foundation has come to a place where in a sense it began. It is transforming the work of individuals and organizations to stand up for nature. Exactly what Philip Gosling did intuitively when he was one of the founders of the

Bruce Trail. He recruited and mobilized individuals to create the clubs that would make a trail that would bring people to nature and then act to protect the Niagara Escarpment.

The idea that experiences with nature can be the seed of a life of adventure and action for nature has proven to be real. The motivation inspired by the song of a warbler singing at Billy Bear camp proves the point.

The Gosling foundation has supported and partnered with many organizations.

National Organizations
Bee City Canada
Birds Canada
Child and Nature Canada
Coalition for Action on Toxics
Canadian Parks and Wilderness Society
Ducks Unlimited Canada
Earth Rangers
Ecojustice
Environmental Defence
Environmental Funders Canada
Fatal Light Awareness Program
Freshwater Future Canada
Green Budget Coalition
Green Teams of Canada
Key Biodiversity Areas Project
Land Trusts Canada
Nature Conservancy of Canada
Sierra Club Canada
Stand
Sustainability Network
Watershed Canada
World Wildlife Fund -Canada

Provincial Organizations
BC Nature
Be the Change Earth Alliance
Bruce Peninsula Sportsmen's Association
Bruce Trail Conservancy
Camp Kawartha
CPAWS BC chapter Canadian Parks and Wilderness Society,
Manitoba Chapter
Carolinian Canada Coalition
Conservation council of New Brunswick
Dogwood British Columbia
Institut Québécois de la biodiversité
Land Conservancy of British Columbia
Land Trust Alliance of British Columbia
National Farmers Union -Ontario
Nature Kids BC

Nature Alberta
Nature Manitoba
Nature New Brunswick
Nature Saskatchewan
Nature Trust of British Columbia
Northern Spotted Owl Breeding Program
Nova Scotia Nature Trust
Nova Scotia Nature
PEI Island Trust
Quebec Nature
Québec natural history research collections
Ontario Farmland Trust
Ontario Nature
Ontario Land Trust Alliance
Ontario Turtle Conservation Centre
Rain Coast conservation Society, BC
Société pour la nature et les parcs du Canada - section Québec
Yukon Conservation Society

Centers and Regional and Local Organizations
Algonquin to Adirondacks Collaborative
Alternatives Journal
Arboretum University of Guelph
Arts Junction
Atlantic Canada Conservation Data Centre
Battle River Watershed Alliance, Alberta
Big Brothers Big Sisters of Guelph
Bruce Peninsula Biosphere Association
Bruce Peninsula Bird Observatory
Burns Bog Conservation Society
Cheakamus Foundation for Environmental Learning
Catsjustwannabecats
Chouette à voir!
Citizens Concerned about the Future of the Etobicoke Waterfront
Couchiching Conservancy

Conservation Halton Foundation
Conservation Manitou
Cowichan Estuary Nature Centre
Credit Valley Conservation Foundation
Creston Valley Bird Fest
Ecologos Water Docs
Ecology Ottawa
Edmonton and Area Land Trust
Escarpment Biosphere Conservancy
Essex County Field Naturalists' Club
Everdale Local Food and Nature Trail
Four Credit Integrated Programs -
    Secondary Schools
        Upper Grand District School Board,
        Algoma District School Board,
        Bluewater District School Board,
        Simcoe County District School Board
Faith and the Common Good -outdoor
    Greening Program
Festival of the Wild Child
Fields to Parks Outdoor Education
    Program
Georgian Bay Biosphere
Go Wild-Grow Wild Festival
Green Thumbs Growing Kids
Greening Sacred Spaces
Guelph Community Foundation
Guelph Hiking Trail Club
Guelph Public Library
Haliburton Highlands Land Trust
Hamilton Conservation Foundation
Hamilton Naturalists Club
Harrison Lewis Coastal Discovery
    Centre
Hike Haliburton Festival
Hilliardton Marsh Research and
    Education Centre
Hospice Wellington
Humber Arboretum and Centre for
    Urban Ecology
Huron Tract Land Trust Conservancy,
Kawartha Conservancy
Kawartha Turtle Conservation Centre
Kensington Conservancy
Kids For Turtles
Lake Huron Centre for Coastal
    Conservation
Lake of Bays Heritage Foundation
Lanark County Stewardship council
Land Conservancy for Kingston,
    Frontenac, Lennox and Addington
Laskeek Bay conservation Society
Le Nichoir
Long Point Basin Land Trust
Long Point World Biosphere Reserve
    Foundation
Long Point Bird Observatory
Magnetawan Watershed Land Trust
Mayne Island Conservancy Society
Manitoulin Phragmites Project
Mantis Arts & Eco Festival
Mississippi Madawaska Land Trust
Muskoka Conservancy
Native Territories Avian Research
    Project
Nature Guelph
Nature's Calling Environmental
    Education
Northwest Wildlife Preservation Society
Oakridges Moraine Land Trust
Okanagan Similkameen Conservation
    Alliance
Ottawa Biosphere Ecocity
Ottawa River Keepers
Pelee Island Buzz
Pelee Island Bird Observatory
Pelee Island Community Arts
Prince Edward Point Bird Observatory
rare Charitable Reserve
Reforest London
Réserve de Biosphère de Fundy
    Biosphere Reserve
Rideau Valley Conservation Foundation
Rocky Point Bird Observatory
Royal Botanical Gardens
Salmon Run Festival, Blue Mountain
    Watershed Trust
Saskatoon Nature City Festival
Save Ojibway Prairie
Somenos Marsh Wildlife Society,

South Shore Joint Initiative, Prince Edward County
Sunrise Therapeutic Riding & Learning Centre
Sustainable Eastern Ontario
Swan Lake Christmas Hill Nature Sanctuary
Thames Talbot Land Trust
The Riverwood Conservancy
The Ontario Water Centre
The Otesha Project
Thetis Island Nature Conservancy
The Working Centre
Thunder Bay Field Naturalists
Toronto Bird Festival
Toronto Botanical Gardens
Toronto and Region Conservation
Trillium Waldorf School
Tree Fest Ottawa
Tucker House
Two Rivers Festival -Wellington Water Watchers
University of Guelph -GRIPP
Wild Ontario

GRIPP

Gosling Research Institute for Plant Preservation

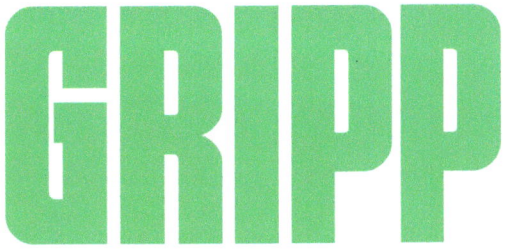

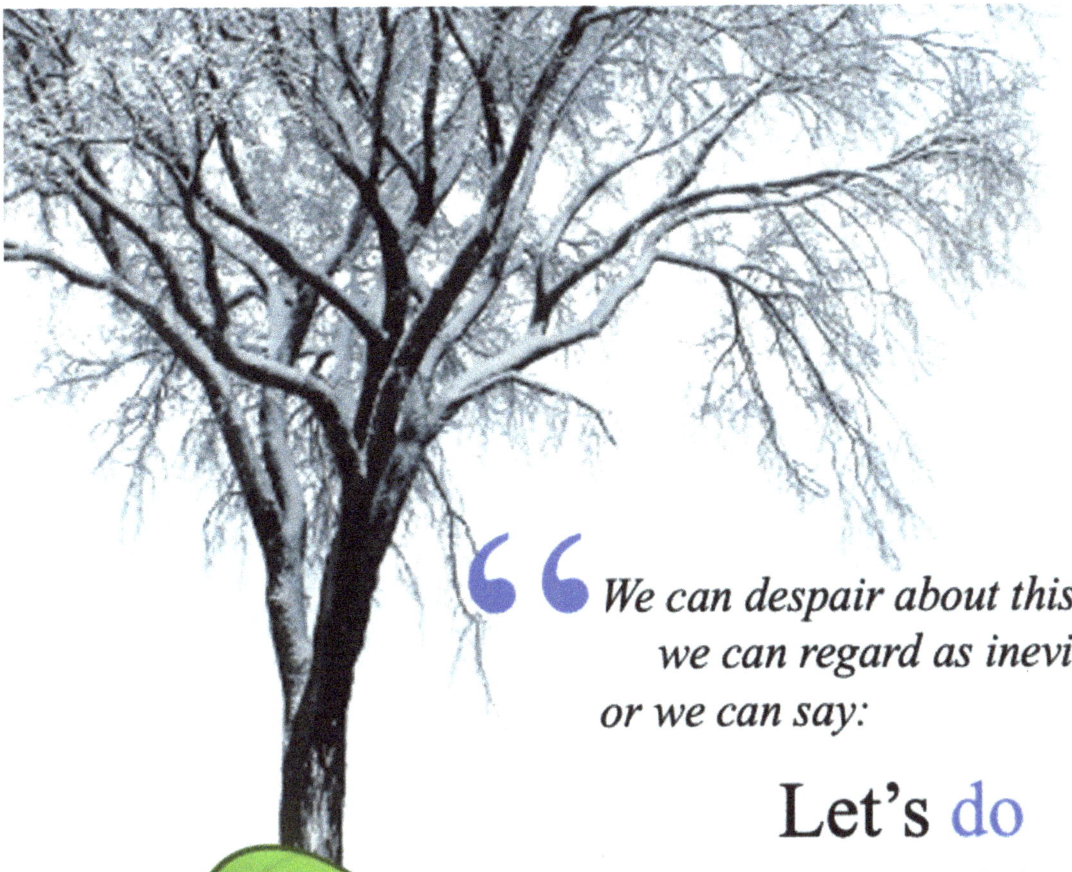

"We can despair about this
we can regard as inevitable,
or we can say:

Let's do
Something,

let's save what we can
while we can."

GRIPP

SAVING ENDANGERED PLANTS

Dr. Philip R. Gosling
Dr. Susan A. Gosling

Dr. Philip R. Gosling & Dr. Susan A Gosling

GRIPP: THE GOSLING RESEARCH INSTITUTE FOR PLANT PRESERVATION

"Save what you can while you can"

Large Elm trees once shaded our garden in Guelph. On their gracious bows, hanging like ladies' purchases, were nests of Orioles, and on summer days their flute-like calls and colorful flight were a constant delight. Then they stopped coming—and we learned about the Dutch Elm Disease.

Walking together at the University of Guelph's Arboretum one sunny afternoon, we came across a research area where American elm tree cuttings were planted and being inoculated with different strains of the Dutch elm disease to test their tolerance. This was a valuable experiment I thought, but Susan said there is a better, more efficient way of propagating an existing tree showing tolerance (only 3% of all American elms are believed to exhibit tolerance).

A friend suggested we contact Dr Praveen Saxena at the University, and we invited him to our house to talk about a possible project. The research he was doing involved tissue culture which lead him to say he would be prepared to take on the challenge of cloning a 100 year old healthy American elm tree (on the campus) something that had never been done before. A couple of hours later Praveen left our house with a commitment to fund his research. In less than a year, that old healthy elm tree was successfully cloned and GRIPP became a permanent research institute at the University of Guelph.

From this important beginning the next step to saving threatened plant species was to cryopreserve living tissue in liquid nitrogen where it would be kept alive indefinitely but thawed and multiplied when needed. Susan`s previous experience in this technology helped convince the TGF Board to donate funds to GRIPP to create a 'Centre for Conservation Research' capable of plant restoration and the ability to 'cryopreserve all of Canada`s plant biodiversity'.

Conservation, Propagation, Redistribution (CPR)
GRIPP's model of saving endangered plants

CPR in the Bruce Peninsula: First success

- In collaboration with Parks Canada, field trials are currently taking place at sites in the Bruce Peninsula Park in order to revive wild populations of endangered species including trees, orchids, and medicinal plants.

- Hill's Thistle (*Cirsium hillii*) is a perennial plant restricted to the Great Lakes Regions of North America and is currently under threat due to habitat loss caused from urban expansion, climate change and encroaching vegetation.

Conservation, Propagation, Redistribution of Hill's Thistle

Spiritual Botany
Connecting Plants, Environment and Spirituality

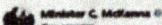

Conserving the Hill's Thistle, @BrucePNP joined @UofG to help this species at risk tackle life in the wild! #ParksCanadaScience @ParksCanada

300 Hills thistle plants regenerated in GRIPP lab were transplanted in 12 different sites in the Bruce Peninsula Park in summer 2017. More than 90% plants survived, thrived, and 30% bloomed.

GRIPP has since evolved into three divisions: research, education and service. In one significant case Parks Canada partnered with GRIPP to save and cryopreserve endangered plants in the Bruce Peninsula. It is called CPR. (Conservation, Preservation and Redistribution.)

Note: 1000 elm saplings were presented to the Gosling Foundation for distribution to cities and towns in Ontario.

TREE HAVEN PROJECT

"How can we save this tiny forest in the city?"

THE TREE HAVEN PROJECT

"How we can save this tiny forest in the city?"

At this time, I live in a wonderful historic stone home in the middle of the city surrounded by trees.

Over the years I have grown to love this place and have never erred from the view that this "tiny forest" should be seen as heritage property protected for prosperity.

But hopes and dreams fade over time and today as I write this final chapter of my BOOK...a new view of the future is needed...thus the "Tree Haven Project."

The challenge now is how to get the city approval for a minimal development... make sure that abundant nature can continue to thrive there, and find a source of income to secure the future cost of long-term site conservation management services of Tree Haven.

For reader's interest, in order to move on, I summarize the work in progress:

- Count and identify the trees (an amazing 729 individual trees were marked and painted.)
- Survey and photo from the air.
- Consider a low-density residential condominium for retirees.
- Prepare a marketing package.
- Confirm the nature conservation message.

Now I must stop!

I believe my tiny forest will be saved (there is much support for this) but in order to finish my book while I still can...I must end here.

"Where all the roads meet" – Scott Galadja.

I hope my writing has been of interest and caused a smile or two but of more importance show how the spirit of volunteerism and love for nature, gave meaning and purpose to my life, and as I wrote at the beginning, "Will serve some useful purpose"

Good, healthy life to all.

Cheers. Philip. The Gosling Charitable Foundation.

"Make no small plans make big plans as small plans have no magic to stir men`s blood." – Daniel Burnham, 1893.

THANKS

It is with some relief at my age (94) to reach the end of my stories. I hope they have been an easy read and an inspiration to many... to follow their own untrodden paths and, in the end, hope they will record their own journey to serve some useful purpose.

I must give my sincere thanks to special people who have encouraged and helped guide me by their quiet presence and approval over the years.

Bob Berry, Lucy Fish, Susan Gosling. Stan Kozak, (Directors of The Gosling Foundation Board), and for their individual contributions, Susan Gosling for her work and promise of saving plant species in the Gosling Research Institute for Plant Preservation (GRIPP). Stan Kozak for his wonderful work as Executive Director of the Gosling Foundation focused on energizing the `Nature Sector` across Canada.

...and my most grateful thanks must go to Barry Scutt...old friend, illustrator and computer expert? who I declare without his constant help and encouragement this BOOK would never have been written.

Philip R Gosling

www.ingramcontent.com/pod-product-compliance
Lightning Source LLC
Chambersburg PA
CBHW061116170426
43198CB00026B/2994